THIS BOOK BELONGS TO...

Name:

Favourite pl.

2019/2020

My Predictions...	Actual...
The Rams' final position:	
The Rams' top scorer:	
Championship Winners:	
Championship top scorer:	
FA Cup Winners:	
EFL Cup Winners:	

Contributors: Peter Rogers

A TWOCAN PUBLICATION

©2019. Published by twocan under licence from Derby County Football Club.

ISBN: 978-1-911502-63-0

£9

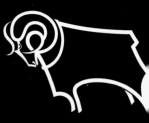

CONTENTS

DERBY COUNTY
FOOTBALL CLUB 2019/20

BACK L-R: Lee Buchanan, Chris Martin, Kieran Dowell, Max Bird, Mason Bennett, Craig Forsyth, Martyn Waghorn, Jayden Bogle, Louie Sibley, Graeme Shinnie, Ikechi Anya.

MIDDLE L-R: Max Lowe, Tom Lawrence, Scott Malone, George Evans, Richard Keogh, Curtis Davies, Henrich Ravas, Jonathan Mitchell, Kelle Roos, Ben Hamer, Tom Huddlestone, Florian Jozefzoon, Matt Clarke, Krystian Bielik, Andre Wisdom, Morgan Whittaker.

FRONT L-R: Jack Marriott, Jason Knight, Liam Rosenior, Shay Given, Phillip Cocu, Chris Van der Weerden, Twan Scheepers, Jamie Paterson, Duane Holmes.

RICHA
KEOGH
6

THE LEGEND
CRAIG BRYSON

Having joined the Rams from Kilmarnock in the summer of 2011, midfielder Craig Bryson wasted little time in making his mark at Pride Park. He netted his first goal for the club to seal a 1-0 Championship victory away to Blackpool in August 2011. Bryson featured in the first four games of 2011/12 as the Rams took a maximum twelve points from their opening four games.

Bryson netted his first career hat-trick as the Rams cruised to an emphatic 5-1 win away to Millwall at the New Den in September 2013. His first goal came on the stroke of half-time to give the visitors a two-goal lead and he completed his treble with further strikes after 57 and 81 minutes.

When Derby County found themselves 4-1 down at half-time at home to Ipswich Town in October 2013, Bryson inspired an unlikely comeback with two goals to help the Rams secure a valuable point. He reduced the arrears just two minutes into the second half and after Jamie Ward hauled the hosts right back into the contest, Bryson was on hand to net a memorable equaliser two minutes from time.

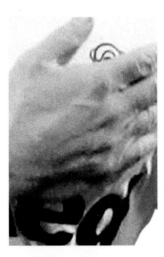

Bryson wrote his name into Rams folklore with a never-to-be-forgotten hat-trick as the Rams handed out a five-goal thrashing to arch-rivals Nottingham Forest in March 2014. The Scot struck first after six minutes and again after 32. Further goals from Jeff Hendrick and Johnny Russell made it 3-0 and 4-0, before Bryson completed his treble from the penalty spot.

The 2013/14 season was certainly Craig Bryson's standout campaign in a Derby shirt with the all-action midfielder netting 15 Championship goals as the Rams reached Wembley for the Play-Off final. Despite his best efforts as a substitute in the Wembley final, he was unable to help the Rams edge past Queens Park Rangers.

After 228 appearances in a Rams shirt and 42 goals, Bryson returned north of the border after agreeing a switch to Scottish Premier League side Aberdeen in the summer of 2019.

MASON BENNETT

2018/19 GOAL OF THE SEASON

10

Derby County academy graduate Mason Bennett won the club's Goal of the Season award for 2018/19 for his stunning acrobatic effort against Wigan Athletic on 5 March 2019.

It was a real case of cometh the hour, cometh the man, as not only was Bennett's strike against the Latics breathtaking in its execution, but it arrived at a moment in the season when the Rams were in serious need of a goal.

Trailing 1-0 at home to lowly Wigan, Derby had lost their three previous Championship matches and were in desperate need of victory to get their Play-Off push back on track. So with the home side a goal behind and fans fearing a repeat of Millwall's 1-0 win at Pride Park in the previous home game, Bennett picked the perfect moment to level with his sumptuous first-time finish.

The stunning volley left visiting goalkeeper Jamie Jones grasping at thin air and arrived just five minutes after Bennett had entered the fray as a 57th minute replacement for Florian Jozefzoon. Not only did Bennett's wonder-strike level the match, but also changed the entire mood inside Pride Park and provided the platform for the Rams to go on and take all three points, thanks to Scott Malone's winner twelve minutes from time.

This goal was one of three that the young attacker netted in the Rams' exciting 2018/19 Championship adventure. His other goals also came at Pride Park in victories over Birmingham City and West Bromwich Albion.

THE SHORTLIST

Rams fans were offered three options when voting for their team's 2018/19 Goal of the Season.

Mason Bennett's stunner was joined by Harry Wilson's outstanding free-kick against Manchester United in the thrilling League Cup triumph at Old Trafford in September 2018 and the third option was Craig Bryson's early opener in the 2-1 Pride Park victory over Sheffield United on 20 October 2018.

Both goals were serious rivals to Bennett's acrobatic effort with all three strikes living long in the memory for Rams fans.

Wilson's free-kick was a moment for individual brilliance while Bryson's goal capped off a stunning team-move to give Derby a 19-second lead en route to victory over the Blades.

Andre WISDOM   2

POSITION: **Defender**   COUNTRY: **England**   DOB: **9 May 1993**

Andre Wisdom's appearances for Derby County in the 2018/19 season were limited to only 13 due to a number of injuries and the emergence of young full-back Jayden Bogle. He signed permanently from Liverpool in 2017 after nearly a decade at Anfield during which he made 22 appearances for the Reds, but he gained most of his experience on loan. Along with Derby, he also spent time with WBA and Norwich City in the Premier League, while he joined up with Austrian Bundesliga side Red Bull Salzburg for the 2016/17 campaign. Wisdom also has experience at international level, having represented England at U16, U17, U19 and U21 level.

Graeme SHINNIE   4

POSITION: **Midfielder**   COUNTRY: **Scotland**   DOB: **4 August 1991**

Midfielder Graeme Shinnie joined Derby County from Scottish Premier League side Aberdeen on a free transfer in the summer of 2019. Born in Aberdeen, Shinnie's professional career began at Inverness Caledonian Thistle, making his first-team debut at the age of just 17. He joined Aberdeen in the summer of 2015 and went on to make 181 appearances for the Dons, netting eleven goals, and wearing the captain's armband since 2017. He has also gained Europa League experience with Aberdeen, as well as playing in two Scottish League Cup Finals and one Scottish Cup Final. On the international stage, Shinnie has six Scotland full international caps to his name.

Craig FORSYTH   3

POSITION: **Defender**   COUNTRY: **Scotland**   DOB: **24 February 1989**

A season-ending injury cruelly meant left-back Craig Forsyth missed the majority of the 2018/19 campaign. The defender, who is one of the club's longest-serving players, suffered an anterior cruciate ligament injury in the defeat against Aston Villa at Pride Park last November. The former Dundee, Montrose and Arbroath man became a permanent member of the Derby squad in the summer of 2013 after impressing during a loan spell from Watford towards the end of the 2012/13 campaign. The Scotsman will be looking to put last season behind him as he hopes to force his way into Phillip Cocu's 2019/20 plans.

Richard
KEOGH
6

POSITION: **Defender** COUNTRY: **Republic of Ireland** DOB: **11 August 1986**

Central-defender Richard Keogh enjoyed one of his best seasons in a Derby County shirt during 2018/19. He captained the Rams for the majority of the season due to Curtis Davies' absence through injury, starting every league fixture, and in all competitions for both club and country, he made 65 appearances. During the campaign, Keogh surpassed 300 league starts for the Rams, becoming only the 29th player to do so in the club's history. His form was also recognised by his peers as he was voted the Player's Player of the Season. On the international stage, Keogh was included in Martin O'Neill's squad for UEFA Euro 2016 and he featured in the Green Army's historic 1-0 win over Italy, before starting against host nation France in the last-16.

Krystian
BIELIK
5

POSITION: **Midfielder** COUNTRY: **Poland** DOB: **4 January 1998**

Poland U21 international Krystian Bielik joined Derby County from Premier League Arsenal in the summer of 2019. Bielik joined the Gunners from Polish side Legia Warsaw in January 2015 at the age of 17 for a reported fee of £2.4 Million. The midfielder, who is also capable of playing in defence, starred during a loan spell with Charlton Athletic last season and was an influential figure as the Addicks overcame Sunderland in the Play-Off Final to secure promotion to the Championship. He produced a Man of the Match performance against the Black Cats, with Lee Bowyer's side coming from behind to claim a last-gasp victory. On the international stage, Bielik was part of the Poland U21 side at the 2019 UEFA European U21 Championships.

THE 2019/20 SQUAD

A Chelsea's Spanish skipper

D Wears the Birmingham City captain's armband

Crystal Palace's nickname **E**

Danish Head Coach at Griffin Park **F**

B Do you recognise this Championship club's crest

The Toffees play their home games here **G**

H Longest serving Championship manager and a Millwall legend

Followed Frank Lampard into the hot-seat at Derby County **C**

Foxes' Nigeria international signing who wears No.8 **I**

A

WHO'S WHO & WHAT'S WHAT OF ENGLISH FOOTBALL?

J
Manchester City's Brazilian striker who was part of their 2019 Copa América winning side

K
Polish international midfielder who was ever-present for Leeds United last season

L
This England international has been with the Red Devils since the age of 7

m
The Seagulls' Premier League top scorer last season

Kieran
DOWELL
8

POSITION: **Midfielder**   COUNTRY: **England**   DOB: **10 October 1997**

The in-demand attacking-midfielder joined the Rams on a season-long loan deal from Premier League Everton. Dowell, a product of Everton's youth system, is highly thought of at Goodison Park and was part of the England U20 squad that won the World Cup in 2017. After a season-long loan across the East Midlands at Nottingham Forest during 2017/18, he spent the second half of last season playing a key role in helping the Sheffield United secure promotion to the Premier League. He made 17 appearances for the Blades in total and scored twice, one of which proved to be crucial in the race for promotion in a 1-0 success at West Bromwich Albion. On the international stage, Dowell has represented England at youth level from the U16s through to the U21s.

Jamie
PATERSON
7

POSITION: **Forward**   COUNTRY: **England**   DOB: **20 December 1991**

The Rams added to their attacking options by completing the loan signing of Jamie Paterson from Bristol City on the final day of the 2019 summer transfer window. Paterson, who scored for Lee Johnson's side against Derby at Pride Park Stadium in the 2018/19 season as the sides played out a 1-1 draw, came off the bench for his parent club in their opening-day defeat to Leeds United before linking up with the Rams. He made his Derby debut two days after joining in a 0-0 draw against Swansea City, before making his first start in a Derby shirt in the 1-0 victory at Scunthorpe United in the First Round of the Carabao Cup.

Martyn
WAGHORN

9

POSITION: **Forward**   COUNTRY: **England**   DOB: **23 January 1990**

It was a good first season for Derby County's number nine Martyn Waghorn. He netted 13 goals in 44 appearances in all competitions having been utilised both down the middle and on the wing. He scored some crucial goals too. He netted the opening goal in Derby's 3-1 victory over WBA on the final day of the season which secured their place in the Play-Off places, while he also scored goals at both Stamford Bridge and St Mary's Stadium. He also netted a hat-trick for Derby County in the 6-1 win over Rotherham United in March which made history for the football club. It was the first time Derby had scored six goals at Pride Park Stadium since its opening back in 1997.

THE **2019/20**
SQUAD

THE LEGEND
KEVIN HECTOR

After joining the club from Bradford Park Avenue for a fee of £38,000 back in 1966, ace marksman Kevin Hector celebrated the Rams' 1968/69 Second Division title success with a goal as Brian Clough's men signed off in style with the 5-0 thumping of Bristol City at the Baseball Ground in April 1969.

After playing a starring role in Derby's 1968/69 Second Division success, Hector featured in a historic First Division match at the Baseball Ground in September 1969. Hector was one of four Rams marksmen as Brian Clough's men demolished Tottenham Hotspur 5-0 on the day the old ground recorded its record attendance of 41,826.

Goals flowed for Kevin Hector both home and away throughout his lengthy Derby career. In August 1975, he added Wembley Stadium to his list of scoring venues. Hector beat West Ham United goalkeeper Mervyn Day with a low right-footed shot after 20 minutes to set Dave Mackay's team on their way to Charity Shield success.

Not for the first time in a Rams shirt, striker Hector was the star of the show as Derby brushed aside Irish side Finn Harps in the 1976/77 UEFA Cup. The ace goalscorer netted five times in an incredible 12-0 rout in what was one of the striker's most talked about Derby appearances.

After a two-year spell in the USA, Hector returned to Derby for a second spell with the Rams. He fittingly signed off his Derby County career with his name on the scoresheet again. He netted a memorable 201st and final goal in a 3-2 Second Division victory over Watford in May 1982.

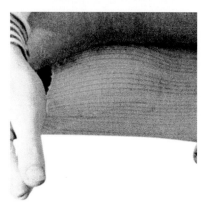

KRYSTIAN
BIELIK
5

Derby County Ladies continued their rise in the Women's game with a record-breaking season that culminated in their highest-ever finish of third in the FA National League Northern Division.

The Ewe Rams finished the campaign with a four-game winning streak to end level on points with second-placed Sunderland Ladies, with only goal difference separating the two sides.

DERBY COUNTY LADIES

Manager Sam Griffiths, in her first season in charge, will move into the 2019/20 season with high hopes of a promotion challenge.

With strengthened ties to Derby County, there was new territory for the club as they faced local rivals Nottingham Forest WFC at Pride Park Stadium in front of a FA National League record crowd of 2,109 fans. Amy Sims, a Rams supporter, headed the only goal of the game to earn a 1-0 victory on the historic occasion.

Ahead of the 2019/20 season, the Ewes will be one of the favourites for promotion after a busy summer with seven new additions. The marquee signings of signings Ellie Gilliatt and Hannah Keryakoplis have added more quality to the squad and have boosted the Ewe Rams hopes.

A second consecutive appearance at Pride Park against Nottingham Forest in early September, highlighted early season and come the end of the campaign, Derby County Ladies will hope to have secured a place in the FA Women's Championship.

Elsewhere across the club, the Development Team regained the Derbyshire FA Women's County Cup with a 4-0 triumph over Long Eaton United Ladies and the Derby County Ladies Academy went from strength to strength with 14 trophies across its youth teams.

The 2019/20 season could end up being a watershed year for the Ewe Rams as they chase their place amongst the elite of the women's game amid the surging popularity of women's football.

Tom LAWRENCE **10**

POSITION: **Forward**   COUNTRY: **Wales**   DOB: **13 January 1994**

Forward Tom Lawrence played 45 games for club and country during 2018/19, netting eight goals, seven for Derby County and one for his country. He scored a dramatic winner on the opening day of the 2018/19 campaign and three for the Rams in the opening month, before netting for Wales in their 4-1 Nations League win over the Republic of Ireland. A boyhood Manchester United fan, Lawrence was handed his senior debut for the Red Devils by current Wales boss Ryan Giggs in a 3-1 win over Hull City at the end of 2013/14. In pursuit of regular first-team football, he joined Leicester City in September 2014 and after loan spells with Rotherham, Blackburn and Cardiff, he enjoyed a breakout year at Ipswich Town. His 11 goals and 11 assists in 2016/17 for the Tractor Boys were key in persuading the Rams to bring him to Pride Park Stadium in the summer of 2017.

Florian JOZEFZOON **11**

POSITION: **Midfielder**   COUNTRY: **Netherlands**   DOB: **9 February 1991**

A lot of Florian Jozefzoon's appearances for Derby County during the 2018/19 campaign were from the substitute's bench, however, he did make two notable and crucial contributions to the season. He scored the winning goal in the dying minutes of the game away at Hull City in September, while in December, he scored the levelling goal against Norwich City at Carrow Road, a game in which the Rams would go on to win 4-3. The Dutch U19 and U21 international, who started his career with Dutch giants Ajax, will be hoping to hit the ground running in the 2019/20 campaign under the stewardship of Phillip Cocu. Jozefzoon has played under the manager before at PSV Eindhoven and will be hoping to make a big impact this season.

Ben
HAMER

12

POSITION: Goalkeeper **COUNTRY:** England **DOB:** 20 November 1987

Goalkeeper Ben Hamer joined the Rams on a season-long loan from Huddersfield Town on the final day of the 2019 summer transfer window and made his debut in the 1-0 win at Scunthorpe United in the Carabao Cup. He began his professional career at Reading and progressed through their youth ranks. After loan spells at Crawley Town, Exeter City and Brentford, he joined Charlton Athletic in August 2011 and excelled as the Addicks were crowned League One champions. After three seasons at the Valley, Hamer joined Leicester City following their promotion to the Premier League in 2014. He acted as cover for Kasper Schmeichel across four seasons, including their stunning title-winning campaign in 2015/16.

Jack
MARRIOTT

14

POSITION: Forward **COUNTRY:** England **DOB:** 9 September 1994

When Derby County signed Jack Marriott in July 2018, they knew he came with a pedigree of scoring goals. His first strike came at Old Trafford as he headed a late goal to put the Rams 2-1 ahead. Derby would go on to win the game on penalties. From that moment, he went from strength to strength, scoring seven goals in ten games including winners against Sheffield United, Sheffield Wednesday and Wigan Athletic. He would also score the winner in an incident-packed 4-3 victory over Norwich City at Carrow Road. He came off the bench in the Play-Off semi-final at Elland Road, and within seconds scored to reduce the arrears, and with time running out, he met a through ball from Richard Keogh and calmly dinked the ball over the onrushing Leeds United goalkeeper to ensure the Rams made it to Wembley.

Matthew
CLARKE

16

POSITION: Defender **COUNTRY:** England **DOB:** 22 September 1996

Matthew Clarke joined Derby County on a season-long loan deal from Brighton & Hove Albion in the summer of 2019, and he went on to make his debut on the opening day of the 2019/20 season as Derby ran out 2-1 winners at Huddersfield Town. Clarke began his career with Ipswich Town and came through the youth ranks at Portman Road. The defender linked up with Portsmouth on loan in August 2015 and spent the entire 2015/16 campaign at Fratton Park, before signing on a permanent basis in the summer of 2016. Clarke's influential role in the Portsmouth side that won the League Two title in 2016/17 and reached the League One Play-Off semi-finals last season, helped him secure a move to Premier League side Brighton & Hove Albion.

FAN

There are five Great Sporting Brits hiding in the crowd... Can you find them?

ANSWERS ON PAGE 62

TASTIC

KIER DOWELL 8

KIERAN DOWELL

8

32Red

Colour in this picture of Rams star Kieran Dowell

Chris MARTIN 19

POSITION: Forward **COUNTRY:** Scotland **DOB:** 4 November 1988

After a year out on loan with Hull City, striker Chris Martin is back with Derby County and hoping to make a telling contribution during 2019/20. Last season, Martin featured 31 times for the Tigers. He scored twice, once in a 6-0 win over Bolton Wanderers and once in a narrow 3-2 defeat against Norwich City. His physical presence, ability to hold the ball up and bring people into play saw Martin become an instant Rams favourite during the 2013/14 season as his 25-goal haul helped the side finish third in the table. Martin went on to score 21 times during the 2014/15 season and that trend continued into a third year as Martin again topped the scoring charts with another 15 strikes for the Rams - the first time that such a feat has been achieved since Dean Saunders between 1988 and 1991.

THE 2019/20 SQUAD

George EVANS 17

POSITION: Midfielder **COUNTRY:** England **DOB:** 13 December 1994

George Evans' start to life at Derby County was unfortunately a cruel one as he suffered a knee injury on his home league debut against Ipswich Town in August. He spent four months on the sidelines which restricted his appearances for the season to just 14 in all competitions. Arguably, his best performance for the club came in the 2-0 victory over Bristol City at Aston Gate in April. The Rams needed to win to stay in the race for a Play-Off spot, but after only eleven minutes, Fikayo Tomori had to leave the field with an injury. In stepped Evans in an unnatural position to put in a man of the match display and help Derby secure a valuable three points. Evans will be hoping to kick on from his injury woes during the new 2019/20 campaign as he looks to cement a starting place in Phillip Cocu's side.

Mason
BENNETT
20

POSITION: Forward   **COUNTRY:** England   **DOB:** 15 July 1996

At just 15 years and 99 days old, Mason Bennett became Derby's youngest ever player when he was named in the starting line-up at Middlesbrough in October 2011, but during the 2018/19 campaign, he really stepped up to the plate, and in his own words stated that it was the best of his career so far. The forward made some match-winning contributions in his opening couple of months. He assisted Tom Lawrence's winner against Reading and also crossed for Florian Jozefzoon to win the game against Hull City at the KCOM Stadium, while his acrobatic effort against Wigan Athletic in March won him the club's Goal of the Season award. He effectively scored the winning goal to seal Derby's passage into the Play-Offs and played a key role in the win against Leeds United. He won a penalty for the Rams in the dramatic 4-3 aggregate win at Elland Road and started in the Play-Off Final against Aston Villa. Bennett will be hoping to go from strength to strength under new boss Phillip Cocu in the 2019/20 campaign.

Kelle
ROOS
21

POSITION: Goalkeeper   **COUNTRY:** Netherlands   **DOB:** 31 May 1992

Five years after signing for the club, Kelle Roos finally made his league debut for Derby County during the 2018/19 campaign, and it proved to be a memorable season for the goalkeeper. He was forced into action following an injury to regular choice Scott Carson. Roos grabbed the opportunity of first-team football with both hands and impressed with a string of superb performances. He went to make 24 appearances and keep eight clean sheets during the season for the Rams in all competitions. The goalkeeper will be hoping to retain the starting position under new manager Phillip Cocu during the 2019/20 season.

The 2018/19 season saw a number of impressive performances from the Rams, here are three to remember...

REWIND

NORWICH CITY 3
DERBY COUNTY 4

The Rams ended the year with a thrilling 4-3 victory away to eventual Championship title-winners Norwich City on 29 December 2018.

In what was one of Derby's most eventful games of the season, the impressive Canaries raced into a 2-0 lead, before goals from Fikayo Tomori and Mason Mount levelled the match at the break.

When Finnish striker Teemu Pukki restored Norwich's lead with nine minutes left, it looked as though the hosts would land all three points. However, in the aftermath of Pukki's goal, one of the Carrow Road floodlights failed and the referee took both teams off the pitch for 20 minutes until the problem was resolved. The Rams must have enjoyed the break for when the action got back underway, Derby turned defeat into victory with late goals from Florian Jozefzoon and Jack Marriott.

DERBY COUNTY 6
ROTHERHAM UNITED 1

Striker Martyn Waghorn was the Rams' hat-trick hero as Derby racked up their most comprehensive win of the 2018/19 Championship campaign with the 6-1 thrashing of Rotherham United on 30 March 2019.

Waghorn opened the scoring from the penalty spot after 13 minutes and from that moment on, the Rams never looked back. Bradley Johnson hit the second before Waghorn netted his second of the game to give the hosts a 3-0 lead at the break.

Mason Mount and Duane Holmes add the fourth and fifth goals before Waghorn wrapped up his hat-trick from the spot after 71 minutes to ensure he left Pride Park with the matchball.

LEEDS UNITED 2
DERBY COUNTY 4

Trailing 1-0 from the first leg of the Play-Off semi-final, Derby County produced an exceptional performance at Elland Road to win the second leg 4-2 on the night, 4-3 on aggregate, and book their place in the Wembley final.

Few gave the young Derby team much hope when Stuart Dallas put Leeds ahead after 24 minutes, but a Jack Marriott goal on the stroke of half-time hauled the Rams right back into the match. A flying start to the second-half saw Derby take control with goals from Mason Mount and Harry Wilson (penalty) putting them 3-1 ahead on the night. Dallas then levelled the aggregate score after 62 minutes, but Marriott's second and Derby's fourth secured an unforgettable victory that will go down in Rams' folklore.

Answer these questions on the *2018/19* campaign and see how much attention you were paying *LAST SEASON!*

1. Who made the most League appearances for the Rams last season?

ANSWER

2. Who netted Derby County's first Championship goal last season?

ANSWER

3. How many points did Derby County finish the 2018/19 season with?

ANSWER

4. How many League goals did the Rams score last season (excluding Play-Offs)?

ANSWER

5. What was the highest home attendance of 2018/19?

ANSWER

6. Against which three clubs did the Rams hit four league goals (excluding Play-Offs)?

ANSWER

7. Who scored the winning penalty in the EFL Cup win at Manchester United?

ANSWER

8. Who knocked Derby County out of the FA Cup in the fifth round?

ANSWER

9. Who received the most yellow cards in the league last season?

ANSWER

10. Who was the only player to receive a red card in the league during 2018/19?

ANSWER

11. Who did the Rams sign from LA Galaxy during the January transfer window?

ANSWER

12. Who top-scored for the Rams in the league last season?

ANSWER

ANSWERS ON PAGE 62

31

FAST FORWARD

There are lots of exciting games ahead for the Rams in the second half of the 2019/20 Championship campaign.

Here are three potential crackers...

STOKE CITY (H)
1 February 2020

After failing to make an impression on the promotion scene under Gary Rowett last season, Stoke City will be hopeful of finding themselves pushing for a return to the Premier League under new boss Nathan Jones.

The Potters still boast a squad packed with Premier League quality and will certainly be looking for a vast improvement on last season's 16th-placed finish.

Derby know from first-hand experience that on their day, the Potters are a match for anyone at Championship level - the Rams lost 2-1 away and drew their home match with Stoke 0-0 last season. This is sure to be an intriguing match-up and a game the Rams will be looking to win.

NOTTINGHAM FOREST (H)
4 April 2020

Pride Park will host the final East Midlands derby of the 2019/20 season when arch-rivals Nottingham Forest visit on 4 April 2020.

April 2020 is a busy month for the Rams and a local-derby triumph would be the best possible way to start an important month at the business end of the season.

With Forest now under the management of Sabri Lamouchi and with three vital Championship points and local bragging right at stake, this really is the standout fixture in the second-half of the season for fans of both clubs. As always, this is certainly one game not to miss!

LEEDS UNITED (H)
25 April 2020

After last season's epic Play-Off semi-final meeting between Derby County and Leeds United, the Championship meetings between the two clubs in 2019/20 were one of the first fixtures that fans looked for back on June 20.

Leeds will provide the Rams' final home opposition of the season when they visit Pride Park for the penultimate game of the season on 25 April 2020. Whether this match provides the level of drama and excitement that season's epic semi-final second leg did - only time will tell!

With two great rivals, who both crave a return to the top flight of English football, going head-to-head, this final home game has all the makings of a classic encounter.

PREMIER LEAGUE

OUR PREDICTION FOR PREMIER LEAGUE WINNERS:
MANCHESTER CITY

YOUR PREDICTION:

OUR PREDICTION FOR PREMIER LEAGUE RUNNERS-UP:
LIVERPOOL

YOUR PREDICTION:

CHAMPIONSHIP

OUR PREDICTION FOR CHAMPIONSHIP WINNERS:
DERBY COUNTY

YOUR PREDICTION:

OUR PREDICTION FOR CHAMPIONSHIP RUNNERS-UP:
LEEDS UNITED

YOUR PREDICTION:

THE FA CUP

OUR PREDICTION FOR FA CUP WINNERS:
WEST HAM UNITED

YOUR PREDICTION:

OUR PREDICTION FOR FA CUP RUNNERS-UP:
MANCHESTER UNITED

YOUR PREDICTION:

EFL CUP

OUR PREDICTION FOR EFL CUP WINNERS:
ARSENAL

YOUR PREDICTION:

OUR PREDICTION FOR EFL CUP RUNNERS-UP:
EVERTON

YOUR PREDICTION:

2020 PREDICTIONS

TEAM WORK

Barnsley

Birmingham City

Blackburn Rovers

Brentford

Bristol City

Cardiff City

Charlton Athletic

Derby County

Fulham

Huddersfield Town

Hull City

Leeds United

Luton Town

Middlesbrough

Millwall

Nottingham Forest

Preston North End

Queens Park Rangers

Reading

Sheffield Wednesday

Stoke City

Swansea City

West Bromwich Albion

Wigan Athletic

Every Championship team is hidden in the grid, except one!
Can you figure out which is missing?

```
A R D N E H T R O N N O T S E R P
D A O V Y U O B S C S A W U T V B
W Y T I C L O T S I R B F E V R N
A V U E R L E Q V P E Y I L C O U
I R M O W C Y U G D E N D A T L L
A P A B J I Z E J L U B H S L G U
T L H I C T X E S A T Y O A S Q T
Q C L G F Y E N V T S F W J K P O
P H U D D E R S F I E L D T O W N
I A F H M A S P V T L N R W X E T
W R D S B M I A O I F U C M Z S O
T L Y K H N E R M Y J Y A I R T W
A T S C A H S K G K L T R K T B N
P O A W R I V R J G N I D A E R R
H N I T A U C A K X U C I E V O L
N A O S O N H N W O L E F W H M P
J T S E B S S G T J C K F J G W N
P H M R N G B E V R V O C Q U I Y
C L V O E B G R A H G T I L O C T
A E B F K V P S E C A S T D R H I
Z T O M S G O E O N I B Y T B A C
V I F A E S F R B U T T E K S L M
O C W H O Q L B N R S F Y N E B A
F U C G B I T Q A R Y X O E L I H
O N H N R A M N W T U M I R D O G
U J A I Y T N U O C Y B R E D N I
N P D T L C V C P I D Z K P I B I
I E G T M S A O D J M F U C M P M
Y N K O X N D H A B O M A S A F R
E D T N O D E T I N U S D E E L I
W I G A N A T H L E T I C B T R B
```

ANSWERS ON PAGE 62

JACK
MARRIOTT
14

Q Ex-Hammer who made his debut for the Golden Boys last season

Middlesbrough keeper who played all 46 league games last season **R**

n France international who joined Spurs from Olympique Lyonnais in July 2019

Joint Premier League top scorer last season alongside teammate Mané and Arsenal's Aubameyang **S**

O Goalkeeper and local lad who came through the ranks at Norwich

Nickname of Yorkshire club Barnsley **T**

The Rams' team kit manufacturer

Former England international in the manager's seat at Craven Cottage **P**

The home of Championship new boys Charlton Athletic **V**

W Managed the Blades to promotion to the Premier League

X Switzerland international who plays his home games at the Emirates Stadium

2019/20 A-Z PART 2

WHO'S WHO & WHAT'S WHAT OF ENGLISH FOOTBALL?

Y The Magpies' international right-back with over 50 USA caps

Z Hammers defender capped over 50 times by Argentina

Max
LOWE
25

POSITION: **Defender**   COUNTRY: **England**   DOB: **11 May 1997**

The 2018/19 campaign was a progressive one for Academy graduate Max Lowe. The left-sided defender spent the season out on loan at Scottish Premiership side Aberdeen as he played with summer recruit Graeme Shinnie. Despite moving to Scotland, a far cry from Pride Park Stadium, Lowe settled quickly and instantly made himself a favourite at Pittodrie. He went on to make 42 appearances for Derek McInnes' side, scoring two goals, and earning plaudits for his attacking intent as well as his defensive solidness. His form was recognised by his peers as he won Aberdeen's Player's Player of the Season award. Lowe will be hoping his time north of the border will help force his way into new manager Phillip Cocu's plans this season.

Duane
HOLMES
23

POSITION: **Midfielder**   COUNTRY: **USA**   DOB: **6 November 1994**

It took a while for Duane Holmes to be presented with his opportunity at Derby County, but when it came, he certainly took it. Signed from Scunthorpe United in August 2018, he joined the club with little fitness following a pre-season injury. It took the midfielder a while to get up to scratch, but he did provide two assists on his debut in a 4-0 win over Hull City in the Carabao Cup. His first league start came in November as the Rams beat Birmingham City 3-1, while his first goal came in January in a 2-1 win over Reading. Holmes went on to make a total of 35 appearances, scoring two goals and assisting four times. Born in Columbus, Georgia, United States, he moved to England aged four. His impressive club form alerted the USA National side and he earned his first cap in a 1-0 defeat against Venezuela.

THE 2019/20
SQUAD

Ikechi ANYA 30

POSITION: **Midfielder**   COUNTRY: **Scotland**   DOB: **3 January 1988**

After spending the majority of the last season in the club's U23 side, Ikechi Anya will be hoping to secure more game-time under new manager Phillip Cocu. Born in Glasgow, Anya began his career at Wycombe Wanderers, but was released as a 17-year-old and entered the non-league system, before returning to the professional game in 2009 with Northampton Town. After heading to Spain to revitalise his career, Anya returned to England on loan, joining Watford in 2012/13 and featured 29 times as the Hornets reached the Play-Off Final. He sealed a permanent switch to Vicarage Road that summer and was a regular in the side that won promotion to the Premier League in 2014/15. He has 29 Scotland caps and has scored three goals, the most memorable against Manuel Neuer and Germany in September 2014.

Curtis DAVIES 33

POSITION: **Defender**   COUNTRY: **England**   DOB: **15 March 1985**

Curtis Davies endured a frustrating 2018/19 campaign as injuries effectively forced him to miss the season. He did start the opening fixture of the season as the Rams beat Reading 2-1, before injury sidelined him. He made a brief comeback in October, but at the end of November he suffered a ruptured achilles against Stoke City that ruled him out for the season. A former England U21 international, Davies has amassed over 500 career appearances to date since making his professional debut at Luton Town where his reputation quickly soared and he became one of England's most sought-after defenders. With a full pre-season under his belt this time around, the defender was raring to go for the 2019/20 campaign under new manager Phillip Cocu.

Jonathan MITCHELL 35

POSITION: **Goalkeeper**   COUNTRY: **England**   DOB: **24 November 1994**

Goalkeeper Jonathan Mitchell had two separate spells out on loan during the 2018/19 campaign. He spent the first half of the season on loan with League One side Oxford United and kept six clean sheets in 15 appearances under Karl Robinson. The second half of the season was spent with fellow League One side Shrewsbury Town. Mitchell made nine appearances and kept four clean sheets. In total, he kept an impressive ten clean sheets from 24 games during the season. He will provide competition this season as the battle for the starting jersey intensifies.

39

LEEDS UNITED
ELLAND ROAD
CAPACITY: 37,890

HUDDERSFIELD TOWN
THE JOHN SMITH'S STADIUM
CAPACITY: 24,500

BLACKBURN ROVERS
EWOOD PARK
CAPACITY: 31,367

PRESTON NORTH END
DEEPDALE
CAPACITY: 23,404

WIGAN ATHLETIC
DW STADIUM
CAPACITY: 25,133

BARNSLEY
OAKWELL
CAPACITY: 23,287

STOKE CITY
BET365 STADIUM
CAPACITY: 30,022

WEST BROMWICH ALBION
THE HAWTHORNS
CAPACITY: 26,850

BIRMINGHAM CITY
ST ANDREW'S
CAPACITY: 29,409

SWANSEA CITY
LIBERTY STADIUM
CAPACITY: 21,088

BRENTFORD
GRIFFIN PARK
CAPACITY: 12,763

CARDIFF CITY
CARDIFF CITY STADIUM
CAPACITY: 33,280

BRISTOL CITY
ASHTON GATE
CAPACITY: 27,000

READING
MADEJSKI STADIUM
CAPACITY: 24,161

MIDDLESBROUGH
RIVERSIDE STADIUM
CAPACITY: 34,742

HULL CITY
KCOM STADIUM
CAPACITY: 25,586

CHAMPIONSHIP GROUNDS 2019/20

SHEFFIELD WEDNESDAY
HILLSBOROUGH STADIUM
CAPACITY: 39,732

Take a look at where the Rams will be heading this season to take on their rivals.

Tick the grounds off once we've visited!

NOTTINGHAM FOREST
CITY GROUND
CAPACITY: 30,445

DERBY COUNTY
PRIDE PARK STADIUM
CAPACITY: 33,597

LUTON TOWN
KENILWORTH ROAD
CAPACITY: 10,356

QUEENS PARK RANGERS
KIYAN PRINCE FOUNDATION STADIUM
CAPACITY: 18,439

CHARLTON ATHLETIC
THE VALLEY
CAPACITY: 27,111

MILLWALL
THE DEN
CAPACITY: 20,146

FULHAM
CRAVEN COTTAGE
CAPACITY: 25,700

TOM
LAWRENCE
10

THE LEGEND
ROY McFARLAND

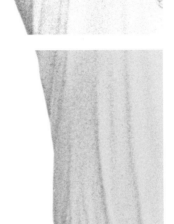

An inspired signing by Brian Clough and Peter Taylor, Roy McFarland arrived at the Baseball Ground in 1967 from Tranmere Rovers. In 1968/69 he formed an impressive partnership at the heart of the Rams' defence alongside Dave Mackay as Derby County landed the Second Division title. The 1968/69 campaign also saw McFarland voted the Rams' Player of the Season.

McFarland stepped up to First Division football with ease and his club performances were rewarded with his first England cap in 1971. Everyone at the Baseball Ground took great pride in seeing their star defender representing his country. McFarland won all 28 of his England caps while at Derby County.

The 1971/72 season was certainly McFarland's finest hour as he captained the Rams to their first-ever Division One title. Forming an outstanding defensive partnership with Colin Todd, McFarland hoisted the Championship trophy aloft after the Rams pipped Leeds, Liverpool and Manchester City to the title by a point.

After leading the Rams to the title in 1971/72, McFarland then helped Derby make their mark on the European stage. The skipper was in the right place at the right time to open the scoring in the European Cup Second Round match against Benfica at the Baseball Ground. McFarland's goal set the team on their way to an historic 3-0 victory over the Portuguese giants.

After a Derby County playing career that saw him amass 530 appearances for the club, McFarland enjoyed a highly successful spell as assistant to Arthur Cox. Under the guidance of Cox and McFarland, the team won successive promotions in 1985/86 and 1986/87 to elevate the club back to the top flight. Roy later succeeded Cox as Rams' boss and led the team to the 1994 Play-Off final at Wembley. A club ambassador, Roy was appointed to the club's board of Directors in 2017.

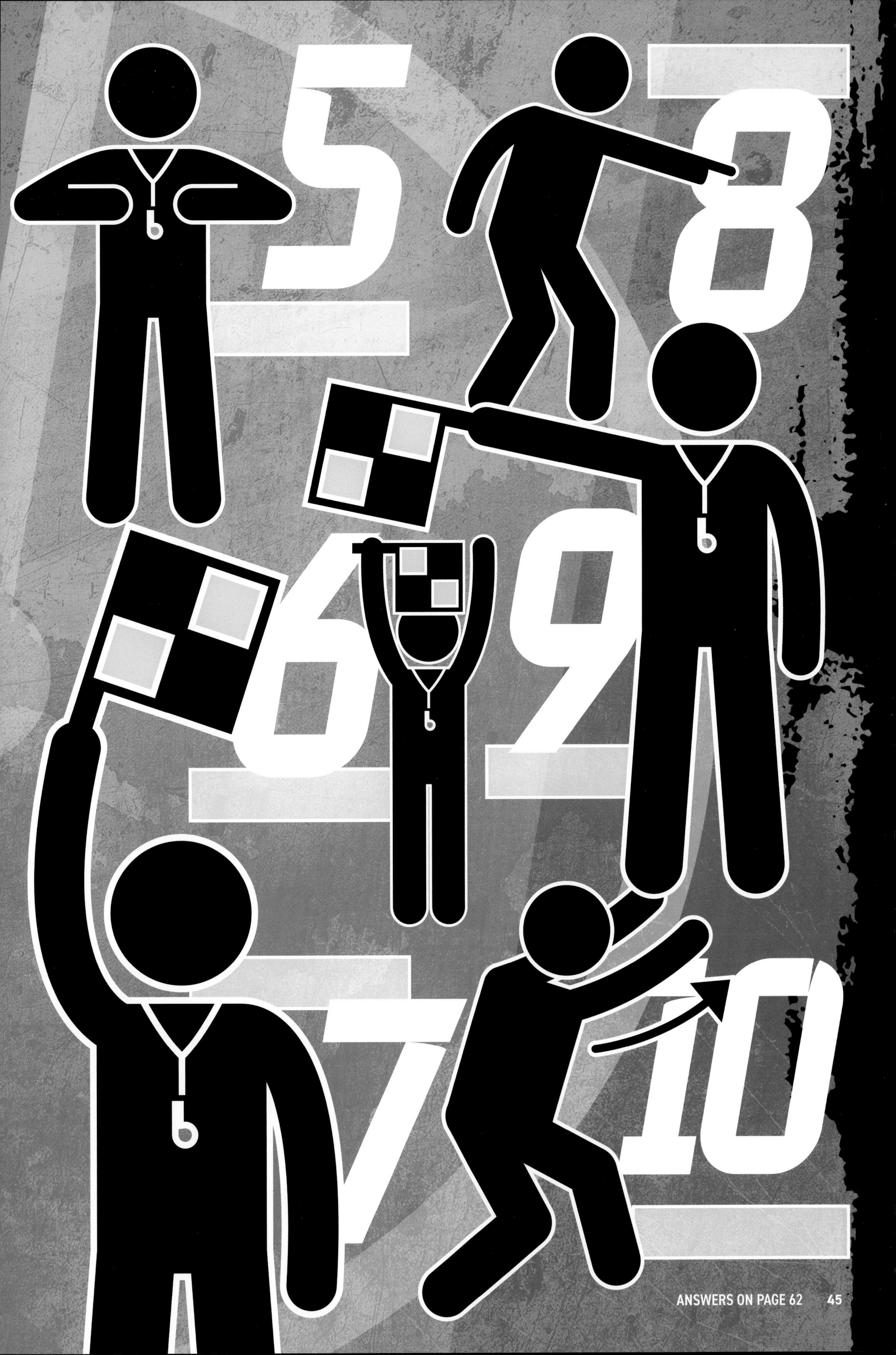
5
8
6
9
7
10

Jason
KNIGHT
38

POSITION: Midfielder   **COUNTRY:** Republic of Ireland   **DOB:** 13 February 2001

Academy graduate Jason Knight had a whirlwind end to the 2018/19 campaign. The midfielder was named as a substitute in the memorable 4-2 victory over Leeds United at Elland Road which secured the Rams a Wembley Play-Off Final place, and he was also named on the bench for that game against Aston Villa. He appeared for the Republic of Ireland U21s at the Toulon Tournament this summer as they reached the Semi-Final stage before being beaten by Brazil. Knight has featured prominently under new manager Phillip Cocu in pre-season and made his professional debut as a substitute on the opening day of the 2019/20 season as Derby ran out 2-1 winners at Huddersfield Town. He went on to make his first-ever career start in the 1-0 Carabao Cup First Round victory at Scunthorpe United just over a week later.

Jayden
BOGLE
37

POSITION: Defender   **COUNTRY:** England   **DOB:** 27 July 2000

After joining the Rams from Swindon Town as a schoolboy, Jayden Bogle's first season in professional football will certainly take some topping. After being handed his debut in the 2-0 win against Oldham Athletic in the Carabao Cup, Bogle made the right-back position his own with a string of impressive displays. Going forward, he recorded some impressive figures. He made nine assists during the season which was the most of any teenager in the league. It was also the most assists for Derby County and for any defender in the league. He also chipped in with two goals. His first in the 3-3 draw at Brentford, while he scored Derby's second in the crucial 2-0 win over Bristol City which helped secure passage through to the Play-Offs. He made 50 appearances in total for the Rams and will be hoping to kick on this season under new manager Phillip Cocu.

Louie SIBLEY

40

POSITION: **Midfielder**   COUNTRY: **England**   DOB: **13 September 2001**

The 2017/18 Academy Player of the Year has been with the Rams since joining the U8s and signed as a first-year scholar at the beginning of 2018/19. Sibley's rise through the academy has seen him become an established member of Darren Wassall's U23 squad and he is now knocking on the first-team door. The versatile youngster, who can play at left-back and all across midfield, has also represented England at U17 and U18 levels in recent seasons. He made his first-team debut under Phillip Cocu after impressing during pre-season, with his bow coming as a substitute in a 1-0 Carabao Cup win at Scunthorpe United.

Max BIRD

41

POSITION: **Midfielder**   COUNTRY: **England**   DOB: **18 September 2000**

It was a memorable 2018/19 campaign for Derby County youngster Max Bird. In only the second year of his scholarship, the Academy graduate appeared for the U18s, stepped up to captain the club's U23 side and trained regularly with the first-team. His impressive displays also earned him some first-team minutes as he appeared in the Carabao Cup wins against Oldham Athletic and Hull City. He made his Championship debut on 1st December in the Rams' 2-1 win over Swansea, while his first professional start for the club came in January against Premier League side Southampton in the FA Cup. In what was a challenging year for the youngster, his efforts were rewarded as he won the Apprentice of the Year at the EFL Awards.

THE 2019/20 SQUAD

Jayden MITCHELL-LAWSON

43

POSITION: **Midfielder**   COUNTRY: **England**   DOB: **17 September 1999**

Jayden Mitchell-Lawson is an energetic and skilful winger who can cause opposition defenders plenty of problems with this technical ability. He was an integral part of the U18 side during his two years as a scholar, before stepping up to the U23s after signing professional terms. The wide-man, who arrived from Swindon Town in 2016 alongside Jayden Bogle, continued to show progress with the U23s and went on to make his first-team debut in March 2019, coming off the bench in a 0-0 draw at home to Stoke City. Capable of playing on either wing, he will be keen to maintain his progress under new manager Phillip Cocu during the 2019/20 campaign.

THE LEGEND
MARK WRIGHT

After winning promotion back to the First Division in 1987, Derby's signing of England international Mark Wright from Southampton certainly demonstrated the club's level of ambition. Wright instantly impressed at the Baseball Ground and was soon installed as club captain. Come the end of the season, it was the team's defensive quality that ensured top-flight survival in 1987/88.

Under the captaincy of Wright, the Rams enjoyed an excellent 1988/89 season as the team improved dramatically. Having finished 15th in the First Division in 1987/88, the side leapt ten places to secure fifth spot in 1988/89. Throughout the campaign, Wright expertly marshalled his teammates and was rewarded with the club's Player of the Season award when he was presented with the Jack Stamps Trophy.

In a testing 1989/90 season at the Baseball Ground, captain Wright was again an influential figure as the team successfully battled against the threat of relegation. Wright's performances saw him voted the Player of the Season and became the first player to win the Jack Stamps Trophy two seasons in a row.

One of two Derby County representatives in England's 1990 World Cup squad, Wright enjoyed a memorable World Cup adventure at Italia '90. He scored his first and only international goal in England's final group game to secure a 1-0 victory over Egypt and ensure Bobby Robson's side entered the final 16 as group winners.

Wright enjoyed a real career highlight towards the end of his time with Derby County when he was handed the England captain's armband as the Three Lions faced the USSR at Wembley in May 1991. The reliable defender was at that stage of his career proudly captain of club and country. After 144 league appearances for the Rams, a big money move to Liverpool followed where Wight captained the Reds to FA Cup glory in 1992. He later managed in the Football League with Chester City, Oxford United and Peterborough United.

DERBY COUNTY F.C.

JAYDEN
BOGLE
37

BARNSLEY

BIRMINGHAM CITY

BLACKBURN ROVERS

BRENTFORD

BRISTOL CITY

CARDIFF CITY

CHARLTON ATHLETIC

DERBY COUNTY

FULHAM

HUDDERSFIELD TOWN

HULL CITY

LEEDS UNITED

In a Rams black and white world, get to know your rivals in full Championship colour!

LUTON TOWN

MIDDLESBROUGH

MILLWALL

NOTTINGHAM FOREST

PRESTON NORTH END

QUEENS PARK RANGERS

READING

SHEFFIELD WEDNESDAY

STOKE CITY

SWANSEA CITY

WEST BROMWICH ALBION

WIGAN ATHLETIC

FIKAYO TOMORI

2018/19

PLAYER OF THE SEASON

Central-defender Fikayo Tomori capped off a great season on loan at Pride Park when he was presented with the Rams' Player of the Season award following a highly impressive 2018/19 campaign.

The on-loan Chelsea star claimed the Jack Stamps Player of the Season award, after his superb displays at the heart of the Derby defence saw the Rams' supporters vote him their club's star performer.

The England Under-21 international featured in a whopping 55 games for Derby as the Rams reached the Championship Play-Off Final at Wembley.

Tomori clearly benefitted from playing alongside the vastly experienced Richard Keogh, who himself was voted the Player's Player of the Season by his Pride Park teammates. Between them, Tomori and Keogh helped the team record 15 clean sheets in all competitions in 2018/19.

The Chelsea loanee's performances certainly propelled his status as one of the most exciting up-and-coming defenders in England.

From the victory at Old Trafford against Manchester United in the Carabao Cup, to the Play-Off Semi-Final victory over Leeds United at Elland Road, the defender was a stand-out member of the Rams squad, and the player himself cherished every minute of his time as a Derby County player.

"It's been the best twelve months of my career so far," confirmed Tomori.

"I've had the best moments I've ever had, and probably ever will have. Some of the nights we have had and some of the games we have played, to finish it off with a Play-Off Final was fantastic, but it would have been nice to have got the win."

YOUNG PLAYER OF THE SEASON

JAYDEN BOGLE

On the night when Fikayo Tomori was crowned the Rams' Player of the Season, at the club's end of season awards event, another talented young defender was also among the awards.

Full-back Jayden Bogle was named the Sammy Crooks Young Player of the Season for 2018/19. The 19-year-old was handed his first-team debut in August 2018 and went on to make the right-back birth his own in the Rams' thrilling 2018/19 campaign.

Reliable in defensive areas, Bogle loves to get forward and contribute to attacking situations. As a result he provided a host of assists in his breakthrough season at Pride Park.

Scott MALONE 46

POSITION: Defender   **COUNTRY:** England   **DOB:** 25 March 1991

Left-back Scott Malone spent the first few months of the 2018/19 season in a battle for the position with Craig Forsyth. Both brought the best out in each other until Forsyth suffered a season-ending injury in November. Malone went on to make 35 appearances for the Rams during the season, scoring two goals. Fighting off competition for his spot in the team from Ashley Cole, he kept his place and helped Derby reach the Championship Play-Offs. The memorable semi-final at Elland Road proved bittersweet for Malone. The full back, already on a yellow card, brought down his man on the edge of the box and received a second yellow, causing him to miss the Play-Off Final against Aston Villa. Malone will be hoping to cement a permanent place in the side during the 2019/20 campaign under new manager Phillip Cocu.

Tom HUDDLESTONE 44

POSITION: Midfielder   **COUNTRY:** England   **DOB:** 28 December 1986

Tom Huddlestone made a total of 31 appearances in all competitions during 2018/19 and surpassed 150 appearances for the Rams. During his first two years at Pride Park, he played 95 games, helped the Rams secure a Play-Off finish and was named in the Championship Team of the Year for in 2004/05. During his eight-year stay in the capital, he lifted the League Cup, played a crucial role in Spurs achieving a Champions League finish and broke into the England set-up - collecting four caps after making his debut against Brazil in 2009. After moving to Hull City in 2013, he helped the Tigers stay in the Premier League and reach the FA Cup Final in his first year and even after they were relegated the following season, the midfielder was a near ever-present as they returned to the top flight at the first attempt, via the Play-Offs.

THE 2019/20 SQUAD

Henrich RAVAS

47

POSITION: Goalkeeper   **COUNTRY:** Slovakia   **DOB:** 16 August 1997

Derby County completed the signing of Slovakian youth international goalkeeper Henrich Ravas in January 2016 and he has made good progress with the club in recent seasons. The Slovakian U19 shot-stopper joined the Rams after spending time with both League One side Peterborough United and National League North outfit Boston United. Ravas linked up with the Rams and immediately joined Derby's U21 squad and played in the last few games to help them lift the Division Two title at the end of 2015/16. Last season, he acted as Derby's third choice goalkeeper, behind Scott Carson and Kelle Roos, and appeared as an unused substitute on several occasions.

Lee BUCHANAN

48

POSITION: Defender   **COUNTRY:** England   **DOB:** 7 March 2001

Lee Buchanan is another exciting player to have progressed through the ranks at Derby County and into the first-team set-up. The left-footed defender, who can play at left-back or centre-back, was part of Derby's U18 side that were National Champions during the 2018/19 season. He was also named as an unused substitute for the Rams' first-team in January 2019 in a home win over Reading, as a reward for his progress at U18 and U23 level. He made his professional bow in the 1-0 Carabao Cup victory at Scunthorpe United in August 2019, and he marked the occasion with a stunning goal at Glanford Park.

Morgan WHITTAKER

49

POSITION: Forward   **COUNTRY:** England   **DOB:** 7 January 2001

Morgan Whittaker had a 2018/19 season to be proud of. The striker scored 24 goals from just 37 appearances for Derby's U18 and U23 teams combined. He also claimed 16 assists, taking his goal contributions for the season to 40. He played a key role in the U18s winning the U18 Premier League North and subsequently becoming National Champions with a 5-2 hammering of Arsenal, in which he scored twice. He was also capped by England at U18. Under new manager Phillip Cocu, he featured with the first-team during pre-season and made his professional debut as a substitute in the side's 1-0 Carabao Cup win at Scunthorpe United.

TOM
HUDDLESTONE
44

56

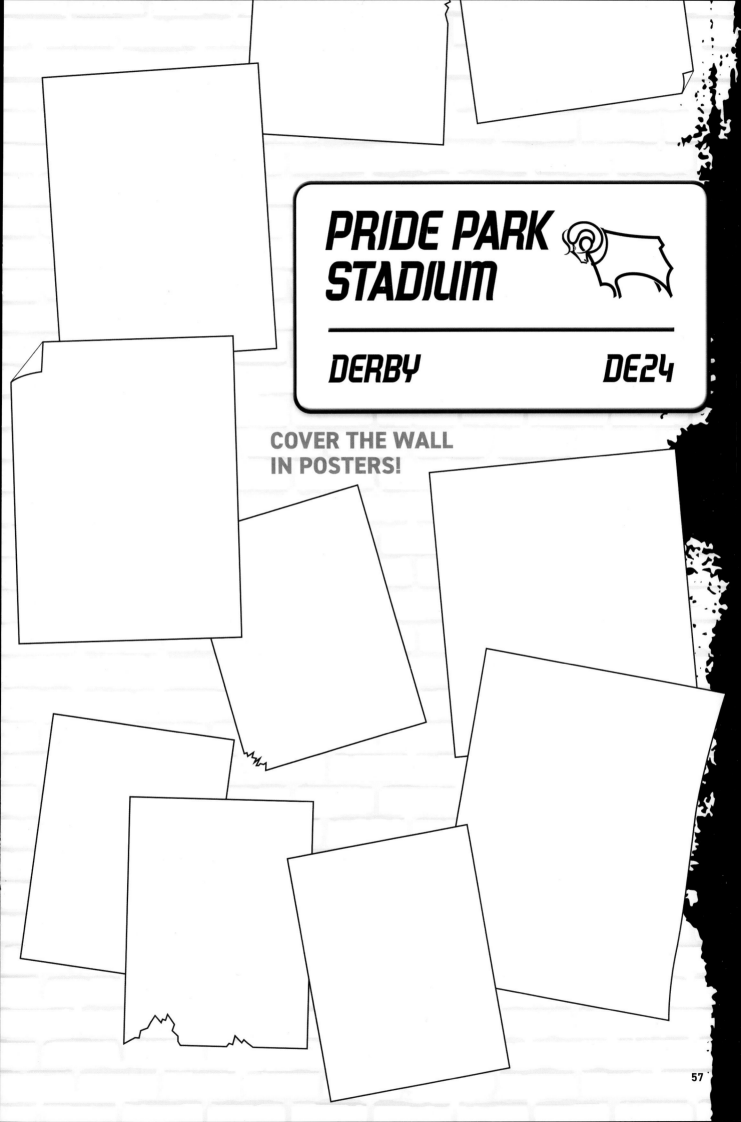

PRIDE PARK STADIUM

DERBY   **DE24**

**COVER THE WALL
IN POSTERS!**

The Rams have boasted a wealth of talent over the years! Here is our...

DERBY DREAM TEAM

...see if you agree!

GOALKEEPER

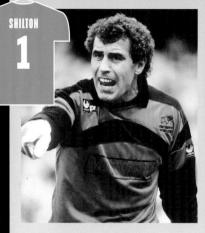

SHILTON
1

PETER SHILTON

Legendary England goalkeeper Peter Shilton made 175 league appearances for the Rams following his move from Southampton in July 1987. A real class act throughout his time at the Baseball Ground, Shilton's vast experience gave great confidence to his teammates.

YOUR CHOICE

DEFENDER

WEBSTER
2

RON WEBSTER

Full-back Ron Webster turned professional with the Rams in 1960 and went on to win three league titles while at the Baseball Ground. He was a Second Division title-winner in 1968/69 and twice a First Division champion with Derby in 1971/72 and 1974/75. Webster amassed an incredible 455 league appearances for the club.

YOUR CHOICE

MIDFIELDER

RIOCH
6

BRUCE RIOCH

All-action Scottish international midfielder Bruce Rioch enjoyed two spells at the Baseball Ground. He was a First Division title-winner in 1974/75 before moving to Everton and then rejoining the Rams in 1977. He captained Scotland in the 1978 World Cup finals and totalled 39 leagues goals for the Rams.

YOUR CHOICE

MIDFIELDER

GEMMILL
7

ARCHIE GEMMILL

Another Baseball Ground legend, skilful Scottish midfielder Archie Gemmill won two First Division titles during his first spell with the Rams. He later played for Nottingham Forest, Birmingham City, Jacksonville Tea Men and Wigan Athletic before returning to Derby as player-coach in 1982.

YOUR CHOICE

FORWARD

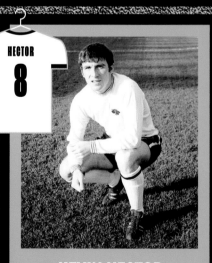

HECTOR
8

KEVIN HECTOR

Signed from Bradford Park Avenue in 1966, striker Kevin Hector remains Derby County's record appearance maker. Like many of his teammates, a First Division title winner in both 1971/72 and 1974/75, Hector also enjoyed two spells at the club and signed off with 201 Rams goals.

YOUR CHOICE

DEFENDER

NISH 3

DAVID NISH

Signed by Brian Clough from Leicester City in August 1972 for a then British record fee of £225,000, David Nish won five England caps while a Derby player. A First Division champion in 1974/75, he scored ten goals in 192 league games for the Rams.

YOUR CHOICE

DEFENDER

McFARLAND 4

ROY McFARLAND

Very much Mr Derby County, Roy McFarland was a Second Division title winner with the Rams in 1968/69. He then formed an outstanding defensive partnership with Colin Todd and captained the club to the First Division title in 1971/72. McFarland played 434 league games for the Rams before returning to the club as coach, and manager.

YOUR CHOICE

DEFENDER

TODD 5

COLIN TODD

After joining Derby from Sunderland, Colin Todd became a standout performer alongside skipper Roy McFarland as the Rams won the First Division title in 1971/72 and 1974/75. England recognition followed, as did the PFA Player of the Year award in 1975.

YOUR CHOICE

FORWARD

SAUNDERS 9

DEAN SAUNDERS

A £1M signing from Oxford United in 1988, Wales international frontman Dean Saunders swiftly repaid his transfer fee by becoming the club's leading scorer during his three seasons at the Baseball Ground. His goals proved vital in securing fifth place in the 1988/89 First Division table.

YOUR CHOICE

FORWARD

GEORGE 10

CHARLIE GEORGE

Recruited from Arsenal in the summer of 1975, England striker Charlie George made his Rams debut at Wembley as the club defeated West Ham United to win the 1975 Charity Shield. George netted 34 league goals for the Rams in 106 league outings.

YOUR CHOICE

FORWARD

HINTON 11

ALAN HINTON

England winger Alan Hinton was the Rams' leading scorer in their 1971/72 First Division title-winning season. He joined Derby County in 1967 and also featured in both the Second Division title success and the club's second Division One triumph in 1974/75.

YOUR CHOICE

TOP 10

MY TOP 10...

MOMENTS OF THIS YEAR

1.
2.
3.
4.
5.
6.
7.
8.
9.
10.

MY TOP 10...

FOOTBALLERS OF ALL TIME

1.
2.
3.
4.
5.
6.
7.
8.
9.
10.

MY TOP 10...

DERBY COUNTY MEMORIES

1.
2.
3.
4.
5.
6.
7.
8.
9.
10.

MY TOP 10...

RESOLUTIONS FOR 2020

1.
2.
3.
4.
5.
6.
7.
8.
9.
10.

MART

WAGHORN

9

QUIZ ANSWERS

PAGE 14 · 2019/20 A-Z PART 1

A. César Azpilicueta. B. Bristol City.
C. Phillip Cocu. D. Harlee Dean. E. The Eagles.
F. Thomas Frank, Brentford. G. Goodison Park.
H. Neil Harris. I. Kelechi Iheanacho.
J. Gabriel Jesus. K. Mateusz Klich.
L. Jesse Lingard. M. Glenn Murray.

PAGE 24 · FAN'TASTIC

Owen Farrell, Lewis Hamilton Johanna Konta,
Anthony Joshua and Ben Stokes.

PAGE 31 · REWIND

1. Richard Keogh, 46.
2. Mason Mount v Reading. 3. 74. 4. 69.
5. 32,055 v West Bromwich Albion.
6. WBA, Norwich City and Bolton Wanderers.
7. Richard Keogh. 8. Brighton & Hove Albion.
9. Harry Wilson, 8. 10. Tom Lawrence.
11. Ashley Cole. 12. Harry Wilson, 15.

PAGE 34 · TEAM WORK WORDSEARCH

Sheffield Wednesday.

PAGE 36 · 2019/20 A-Z PART 2

N. Tanguy Ndombele. O. Aston Oxborough.
P. Scott Parker. Q. Domingos Quina.
R. Darren Randolph. S. Mo Salah. T. The Tykes.
U. Umbro. V. The Valley. W. Chris Wilder.
X. Granit Xhaka. Y. DeAndre Yedlin.
Z. Pablo Zabaleta.

PAGE 44: HEY REF

1. Direct free kick. 2. Indirect free kick.
3. Yellow card - Caution.
4. Red card - Sending off. 5. Obstruction.
6. Substitution. 7. Offside/foul. 8. Penalty.
9. Offside location. 10. Play on.